COUNTRIES OF THE WORLD

SOUTH KOREA

ROB BOWDEN

Evans

TITLES IN THE COUNTRIES OF THE WORLD SERIES:
ARGENTINA • AUSTRALIA • BRAZIL • CANADA • CHILE
CHINA • EGYPT • FRANCE • GERMANY • INDIA • INDONESIA
ITALY • JAPAN • KENYA • MEXICO • NIGERIA • POLAND
RUSSIA • SOUTH KOREA • SPAIN • SWEDEN • UNITED KINGDOM
USA • VIETNAM

Published by Evans Brothers Limited
2A Portman Mansions
Chiltern Street
London W1U 6NR

VISIT OUR WEBSITE
www.evansbooks.co.uk

First published 2006
© copyright Evans Brothers 2006

Produced for Evans Brothers Limited by
Monkey Puzzle Media Limited
Gissing's Farm, Fressingfield
Suffolk IP21 5SH, UK

British Library Cataloguing in Publication Data
Bowden, Rob
South Korea. – (Countries of the world)
1.Korea (South) – Juvenile literature
I.Title
951.9'5043

ISBN 0 237 52855 X
13-digit ISBN (from 1 January 2007) 978 0 237 52855 3

Editor: Clare Weaver
Designer: Jane Hawkins
Photographs by Rob Bowden (images@easi-er.co.uk)
Map artwork by Peter Bull
Charts and graph artwork by Encompass Graphics Limited

Endpapers (front): The sprawling port complex
of Busan, one of the largest and busiest ports
in the world.
Title page: A crowded street in central Seoul.
Imprint and Contents pages: The densely
populated centre of Seoul extends beyond
the Han River to the foothills of the
surrounding mountains.
Endpapers (back): Rice fields dominate this
agricultural valley in the central-western region
of South Korea, near Jeongeup.

The colours of the South Korean flag represent the philosophical idea of yin and yang: blue is yin, which is dark and cold, while red, which is yang, is bright and hot. The four black symbols, called *kwae*, represent heaven, fire, water and earth.

South Korea's capital, Seoul, is a thriving global city and the driving force behind the growth of the whole economy.

South Korea is a country of remarkable contrasts, where ancient palaces are found alongside state-of-the-art skyscrapers, and local traditions co-exist with ultra modern lifestyles. A fast-changing economy, spectacular landscapes, a unique culture and a fascinating history all add to the intrigue of this north-east Asian nation.

GLOBAL LEADER

At the time of its founding as a republic in 1948, South Korea was a predominantly agricultural nation and one of the poorest countries in the world. In remote parts of the country, evidence of this former lifestyle still exists, but for the majority of South Koreans life is now very different. Today, South Korea is a thriving economic force and,

PROVINCES AND MAIN CITIES

besides Japan, the only Asian nation in the Organisation of Economic Co-operation and Development (OECD), a grouping of 30 of the world's leading economies. By focusing on key economic sectors, South Korea has established itself as a global leader in the manufacture of consumer and industrial electronics, in vehicle production and as the world's leading shipbuilder. By 2002, South Korea had become the world's twelfth biggest exporter by value, ahead of economies such as Russia, Spain, Sweden and Australia. Despite a regional economic slowdown in 1997, South Korea has continued its spectacular economic growth, expanding by an annual average of 5.2 per cent GDP (Gross Domestic Product) over the decade to 2003, twice the OECD average.

The impact of South Korea's success is evident far beyond its borders. Many of South Korea's leading manufacturers have become household names across the world, such as the electronics companies Samsung and LG (Lucky Goldstar), and the car producers Hyundai and Kia. The results of this economic turnaround within the country have been incredible. From being one of the world's poorest nations, South Koreans now enjoy a standard of living equivalent to many people living in Europe or North America. In 2003, average incomes in South Korea were equivalent to around 78 per cent of the European and OECD average and higher than those in Greece or Portugal.

The transformation is clear to see in the cities. Evening streets buzz with the noise of people enjoying a night out, shopping arcades heave with bargain hunters, and queues form outside cinemas and theatres. In fact, at first glance, there is little to separate the major cities of South Korea, such as Seoul, Busan and Ulsan from any other large city in the developed world.

KEY DATA

Official Name:	Republic of Korea
Area:	99,268 km^2
Population:	46,835,000 (2000 Census)
Main Cities:	Seoul (capital), Busan, Daegu, Incheon, Ulsan
Official Language:	Korean
GDP Per Capita:	US$17,971*
Currency:	South Korean won (KRW)
Exchange Rate:	US$1 = 1,191 won £1 = 2,024 won

*(2003) Calculated on Purchasing Power Parity basis
Sources: CIA World Factbook, 2004; World Bank

Despite the incredible pace of development in South Korea, traditional culture remains strong.

KINGDOMS AND CONQUEST

For most of its past, South Korea has shared its history with North Korea but, even so, Korea was frequently divided into numerous individual states or kingdoms. These were periodically united by a dominant power before again separating. Korea's history is, therefore, very complex, but it is possible to identify several key periods that have had a lasting impact.

The Three Kingdoms period brought together various tribal states into three rival kingdoms – the Koguryo (founded 37 BC), Paekche (18 BC) and Silla (57 BC). In AD 668, with the support of the Chinese, the Silla kingdom united all of Korea. In the late eighth century, the Silla kingdom again divided into the three kingdoms. In 936, these were replaced by the Koryo kingdom, from which Korea gets its name. The Koryo remained in effective control until 1392, when land

---

The Silla established regional capitals and built grand palaces in the Silla capital (modern-day Kyongju) – many of which survive to this day, such as the magnificent Pulguk Temple.

reforms ushered in the new Choson dynasty – made up of 26 monarchs who ruled until 1910. Throughout this period, Korea faced invasions from Japan and China, but managed to withstand these until 1910, when Japan finally annexed the country. Japanese rule was brutal – resistance was quashed and sweeping changes were brought in to force Koreans into the Japanese way of life.

A COUNTRY DIVIDED

Japanese rule in Korea ended with the 1945 defeat of Japan in the Second World War. Korea came under the control of a temporary international trusteeship – the US military controlled the south, whilst Soviet forces controlled the north. Two opposing governments emerged and the country became divided into opposing political ideologies, neither recognising the other. The Republic of Korea was formed in May 1948, and had the support of Western powers and the United Nations (UN) as the legitimate government in Korea. In the northern part of Korea, the People's Republic of Korea was declared in September 1948, with the support of the USSR. In June 1950, northern troops

launched an attack to take southern Korea by force. This marked the start of the Korean War, which lasted for three years and became one of the major conflicts of the Cold War. The south was militarily supported by the UN, and Chinese forces backed the north. An estimated 4 million Koreans lost their lives during the conflict and the country remains

A joint military parade of South Korean and US forces commemorates the retaking of Seoul during the Korean War.

divided along the 1953 ceasefire line. Today, there are renewed hopes for a unified Korea, but tensions remain strong, with both nations on military alert.

POLITICAL CHANGE

South Korea is today a stable civilian democracy, but from 1961 to 1988 the country was effectively under military rule, though elements of civilian government remained in place. General – and later, President – Park Chung Hee was the principal leader during the military rule era. He initiated the economic transformation of South Korea, but at a cost. Personal freedoms were restricted, and the press and political opposition were suppressed. In 1972, Park rewrote the constitution and gave himself sweeping powers. This resulted in political protests that were violently put down, with hundreds of civilian casualties. Park was assassinated in October 1979 by the head of his own intelligence agency. Calls for a return to full democracy led to a revised constitution in 1980 and the election of Chun Doo Hwan in 1981. The full reinstatement of civilian government took place in 1987 when a national referendum approved yet another new constitution. The civilian government remains in place today, with a president elected by popular vote for a single five-year term.

Much of South Korea is covered in low mountainous terrain, interspersed with fertile farming valleys, such as here, near Jeongeup.

South Korea occupies the southern end of a peninsula that juts southwards from China. The East Sea (Sea of Japan) separates South Korea from Japan to the east, whilst the Yellow Sea separates it from China to the west.

Mountains, river valleys, coastal plains and hundreds of small islands form a diverse landscape, and climates range from subtropical in the south to temperate in the north.

LANDSCAPE FEATURES

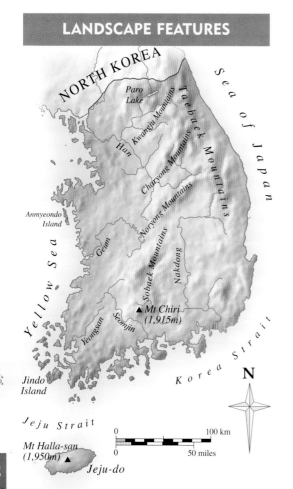

LAND OF MOUNTAINS

South Korea is not a large country, covering a total area of just 99,268km^2 – roughly equivalent to the US state of Indiana or about one third the size of Italy. Of this area, around 70 per cent consists of low mountain ranges – rising to 1,915m on the mainland and to 1,950m at Mount Halla-san, the country's highest point on Jeju-do island. The principal mountain range is the Taebaek (Great White) range that runs in a roughly north-south direction, forming a spine down the eastern flank of the country and continuing into North Korea. The Sobaek (Little White) range branches from the southern end of the Taebaek range and extends in a south-westerly direction across the centre of the country. Three smaller

These basalt columns at Jusangjeolli on Jeju-do provide evidence of the island's volcanic origins. They were formed around 500,000 years ago by the rapid cooling of molten rock.

Whilst most of South Korea's mountains have been formed by geological uplift, the islands of Ulleung-do and Jeju-do are actually extinct volcanoes. Jeju-do is particularly impressive and lies around 100km off the south coast. It is completely dominated by Mount Halla-san (1,950m), a shield volcano that last erupted in AD 1007. Evidence of its volcanic past can be found across the island, with some 400 cinder cones and around 60 lava tubes dotted around. The longest of these lava tubes has formed a cave system over 12km long, making it one of the largest in the world. Jeju-do's volcanic soils are very fertile and the island has a thriving agricultural industry, which, besides vegetables and cereals, also produces tangerines and green tea. The volcano attracts many tourists who venture into the subterranean lava tubes, visit unusual rock formations or hike to the crater-lake Beangnokdam at the summit – South Korea's only natural lake.

ranges – Noryong, Charyong and Kwangju – also branch from the Taebaek range and head westwards. These have been described as the rib bones of Korea, because of the way they connect to the Taebaek spine.

RIVERS

Most of South Korea's rivers begin life amidst its mountainous spine and take one of two distinctive forms, depending on which direction they drain. Those that drain eastwards have a relatively short journey to the East Sea and are steep in nature, carrying rainwater swiftly away from the mountains and drying up at other times. By contrast, those that flow westwards or southwards are longer and slower rivers that follow the gradual fall of the Korean peninsula into the Yellow Sea. The most significant rivers in South Korea are all of this latter type and include the Han River (514km) that flows through the capital Seoul, the Nakdong (525km), the Geum (401km) and the Seomjin River (212km).

ABOVE: A cruise boat carries tourists on Soyang Lake, near Chuncheon. The lake was formed in 1973 by the completion of Soyanggang Dam across the Soyang River.

RIGHT: The Yeongsan River Dam near Mokpo is 4,300m long and was built in the late 1980s. It protects upstream areas from the intrusion of tidal waters at high tide.

LIVING WITH RIVERS

The irregular flow of South Korea's rivers means they are not suited to river transport – except in their very lower stages – and only then by small vessels. To improve the regularity of their flow, dams have been built across most of South Korea's rivers, forming numerous artificial lakes. In addition to preventing flooding – by controlling the release of water downstream – the dams also store water for irrigation and the generation of hydroelectric power (HEP). The storage lakes have also become popular recreational areas for tourists.

The west coast of South Korea experiences one of the highest tidal ranges in the world, with high and low water levels varying by as much as 8.5 metres. One effect of this is a reversal in the flow of several west coast rivers at high tide. To protect cropland and prevent flooding in estuary regions, tidal barrages have been built on some of the most affected rivers, including the Geum, Sapgyo and Yeongsan. These barrages prevent salt-water intrusion and store fresh water until it can be released at low tide. New farmland has been created on the upward side of the barrages by reclaiming former tidal flats. The freshwater storage lakes formed by the barrages are also used for recreation.

COASTS AND ISLANDS

The east coast of South Korea is predominantly smooth, with only one large inlet at Pohang and several smaller inlets at Ulsan, Donghae and Sokcho. Besides these, the coastline rises sharply from the sea into the Taebaek mountains. The southern and western coastline is, by contrast, heavily indented with numerous bays and inlets concealed between jutting peninsulas. River estuaries on the west and south coasts give way to coastal plains that continue inland as floodplains along the course of the country's major rivers. This land is heavily populated and is where most of South Korea's large settlements and farmland are found. In addition to natural plains, several artificial plains have been created through land reclamation from shallow tidal waters on the west coast. This process is continuing today with the Saemangeum Project (see page 54) – one of the world's biggest land reclamation projects.

Off the southern and western coastlines of South Korea are thousands of islands – the visible portion of hills and mountains that are slowly sinking into the sea. The majority of

ISLANDS

South Korea has around 3,000 islands, the majority of which are located off the south-west coastline. The province of Jeollanam-Do alone has some 2,000 islands, including 1,700 that make up the Dadohae Marine National Park – the largest in the country.

these islands are small and uninhabited, but at least 400 of the larger islands host small fishing communities and are increasingly popular with tourists. Inhabited islands are connected to the mainland by ferry services or road bridges for those very close to the mainland.

Vast tidal mudflats are exposed at low tide near Buan on the west coast. Clams and other shellfish are harvested from the mudflats.

CLIMATE AND WEATHER

South Korea's climate is heavily influenced by its proximity to the continental landmass of Asia and by the seas that surround it. In general, it could be described as a temperate climate with four distinct seasons, similar to that of the UK. Long winters and summers are punctuated by much shorter spring and autumn seasons that are considered the most pleasant times of the year. Winter begins in November and is marked by cold air moving south from Siberia and Manchuria (China). By December and January, average temperatures have dropped to below 0°C over the whole country, with the exception of some coastal regions and Jeju-do. In Seoul, winter temperatures regularly drop to –8°C and have been known to reach –24°C.

By the end of March, winter draws to a close, and a short spring starts as warm air begins to move northwards from the Pacific Ocean. Temperatures typically average 10 to 12°C and rainfall is unpredictable, dependent on weather systems travelling eastwards from China. The spring rains are important for the planting of rice, and when they have failed in the past, there have been serious food shortages and even famine.

By the end of May, summer ushers in a period of warm air and heavy rainfall that lasts until the end of September. South Korea typically receives around 1,250mm of precipitation a year and around 60 per cent of this will fall as rain during the summer months. In general, the south and west are wettest. Southern Jeju-do receives the highest average rainfall of around 1,700mm per year. Summer temperatures in South Korea average around 25°C, but can regularly approach 30°C in July and August.

CLIMATE

Key
11 average annual temperature (°C)

TEMPERATURE AND RAINFALL

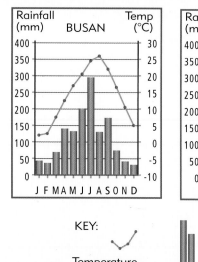

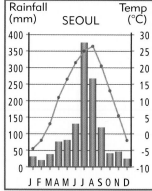

KEY:

Temperature   Rainfall

PRECIPITATION

NORTH KOREA

Sea of Japan

1300
1200
1100
Chuncheon
1500
1400
1300
Incheon   Seoul
Suwon
1200

SOUTH KOREA

Cheongju
1100
1000
1300

Daejeon
Gunsan

Daegu

Jeonju
1300
1400
1500
Ulsan

Gwangju
1500
1600
1700
Busan

Mokpo
1400

1500

Yellow Sea

N

0   100 km
0   50 miles

Jeju
1600
1700
Jeju-do

Key
1100 average annual
      precipitation (mm)

The combination of high temperatures and rainfall makes the summer months very humid, with August being an especially uncomfortable month. An additional feature of the summer months is the risk of typhoons welling up from the Pacific. By the time they reach South Korea they have normally lost most of their strength, but periodically a severe typhoon will strike – causing flooding, structural damage and some loss of life. The worst typhoon to strike the country in modern times occurred in 1959, with 849 people being killed.

By mid-September, cool dry northern winds from Siberia again begin to influence weather patterns. Autumn temperatures fall to around 15°C and the skies are clear and crisp for several weeks, with only the occasional shower. Koreans consider this the most pleasant season, particularly as the hillsides become a dazzling display of spectacular autumn colours. Autumn is also the time of several public holidays, the most important of which is *Chuseok*, when families return to their ancestral homes and give thanks for the harvest from the earth.

The Taebaek mountains become a riot of colour during the autumn and attract hundreds of thousands of tourists to marvel at nature's display.

POPULATION AND CHANGE

A sea of faces in central Seoul – one of the most densely populated cities in the world.

Since the end of the Korean War, the population of South Korea has increased dramatically. By 2004, it was the world's 24th most populous country. The nature of the population has also changed. More people are living in urban areas and the population is ageing as people live longer and births decline.

A POPULATION BOOM

At the outset of the Korean War in 1950, South Korea had a population of around 18.9 million people – of whom over a million are thought to have died during the war (exact figures are not known). The post-war period witnessed rapid population growth, as high birth rates coincided with lower mortality rates due to medical advances, such as antibiotics. Between 1955 and 1960, the population expanded by over 3 per cent per year, causing a baby boom. By 1960, the population had reached 25 million – more than that of the entire Korean peninsula prior to its division.

Realising the potential pressure on living conditions and food production, the South Korean government introduced intensive family planning policies in the early 1960s. At the same time, South Korea experienced a period of rapid economic growth and modernisation. This led to later marriages and a natural inclination towards smaller families. This social change was triggered by a new

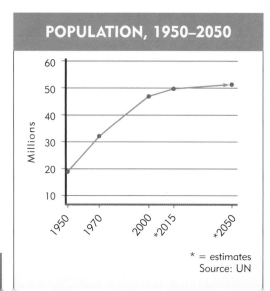

POPULATION, 1950–2050

Millions (y-axis: 10, 20, 30, 40, 50, 60)

x-axis: 1950, 1970, 2000, *2015, *2050

* = estimates
Source: UN

South Koreans are starting their families later in life and limiting themselves to just one or two children on average.

481 people per square kilometre (km²). Mountainous areas in the north and east are considerably less populated, with densities typically below 50 people per km². By contrast, major urban centres have population densities that are typically higher than the national average. Busan, for example, had a population density of over 4,800 people per km² according to the 2000 census. A particular characteristic of South Korea's population distribution is the overwhelming pre-eminence of the capital city Seoul. Figures from the 2000 census show that just under 22 per cent of South Koreans live in Seoul, giving it a population density of over 16,300 people per km² – among the highest in the world.

cultural value, whereby people came to accept that 'the less children you have, the better off you are'. By 1970, population growth had slowed to 2 per cent and fell further to around 1.5 per cent during the 1980s. By 1990, however, South Korea's population had reached around 43 million and, although growth slowed further to less than 1 per cent per year, the population had topped 48 million by 2004. South Korea's population is now entering a period of stability and is likely to grow only slowly over the coming decades, if at all. Different estimates for the year 2050 place the population at somewhere between 46.4 and 51.3 million. Reunification with North Korea would more than likely disturb this period of stability as North Koreans moved south to benefit from the higher standards of living in present-day South Korea.

POPULATION DENSITY

Due to its small size and large population, South Korea has one of the highest average population densities in the world at

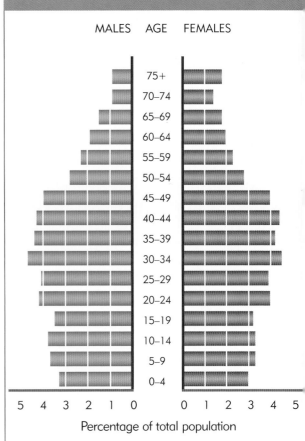

POPULATION STRUCTURE, 2004

Source: US Census Bureau

URBANISATION

New apartments being constructed in Suwon, one of the main satellite cities of Seoul.

South Korea is one of the most urbanised countries in Asia – with 80 per cent of people living in urban areas in 2003. This compares to 65 per cent in Japan and just 39 per cent in China. The urbanisation of South Korea has taken place very rapidly. In 1950, only 21 per

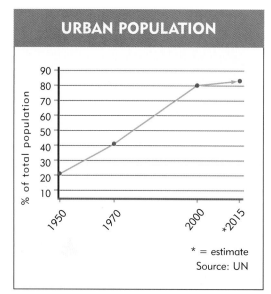

cent of people lived in urban areas, but by 1975 this had more than doubled, to 48 per cent. The 1960s experienced especially swift urbanisation. A series of five-year economic plans (beginning in 1962) created rapid industrialisation and thousands of new job opportunities. At the same time, population growth was placing agricultural land under increasing pressure, so many people opted to move to the cities. During the 1970s, rural-urban migrants accounted for 55 per cent of the population growth in urban areas.

Seoul and Busan bore the brunt of urbanisation during the 1960s and 1970s – their populations growing by 350 and 270 per cent respectively between 1960–80. Their growth slowed in the 1980s and both cities have seen a decline in population since the 1990s. This decline is explained by the growth of satellite towns and cities. These developed as land in the principal cities became scarce and the cost of housing made it prohibitive for new migrants to live there. The satellite settlements offer cheaper housing and are well connected to the major cities by urban rail and bus services. Incheon and Suwon, for example, have become key satellite cities of Seoul and have more than doubled in population since 1985.

POPULATION REDISTRIBUTION

Although central Seoul has witnessed a gradual out-migration of people since the late 1980s, most have only moved into the immediate environs. As a result, South Korea's population remains extremely unbalanced, with just under half of all people living in the Seoul metropolitan area. This area today extends outwards some 40–50km from central Seoul. Since the late 1970s, the government has been trying to encourage a redistribution of population away from the Seoul area, but generally this has had little success. Some new industrial complexes, such as the steelworks at Pohang, and the chemical works at Ulsan, have succeeded in attracting significant numbers of people to the south-east of the

country. It is here that the industrial port city of Busan is situated. Around 30 per cent of the South Korean population now lives in this south-east urban area. The metropolitan area around Seoul continues to grow, however, and the government will need to do much more if it is to entice people to settle in other provincial cities.

CASE STUDY
NEW SONGDO CITY

Around 64 kilometres to the south of Seoul, a new hi-tech industrial city is being created on 600 hectares of land reclaimed from the Yellow Sea. By around 2015, Songdo will house major international companies, a conference centre, leisure and retail facilities and homes for around 200,000 people. With close connections to Incheon International Airport (the main gateway to South Korea) and improved seaport facilities, Songdo is set to become a major new urban growth pole during the twenty-first century.

Most of South Korea's urban population lives in high-rise apartment complexes – such as these in Mokpo.

AGEING SOCIETY

In 1960, only 3 per cent of South Korea's population was aged over 65 and life expectancy was around 56 for women and 53 for men. Today, improvements in living conditions and in medical care mean that life expectancy is 78 for women and 71 for men. By 2003, the proportion of the population over 65 years of age had reached 8 per cent. In real terms, this represents an increase in the elderly population (those over 65) from 0.75 million people in 1960 to 3.83 million by 2003. Current trends suggest that South Korea's society will age even faster in the coming decades, with 14 per cent of the population being over 65 years of age by 2019 and 20 per cent by 2026. This equates to an elderly population of some 10 million people.

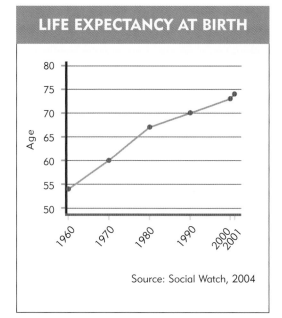

LIFE EXPECTANCY AT BIRTH

Source: Social Watch, 2004

The elderly in Korean society are traditionally cared for by their children. Parents would spend their earnings and savings to help their children to establish their own lives and, in return, expect to be cared for in their later years. This pattern is changing under the pressures of modern life, higher living costs and longer life expectancies. Around 45 per cent of South Koreans, for instance, now live far away from their parental homes, making it harder for them to care for their parents in old age. Parents, too, are taking the active decision to remain independent of their children and instead opting to settle in so-called 'silver towns' when they retire. To fund this change in lifestyle, parents are now saving money whilst working, whereas traditionally they would have spent any income on their children. Many elderly people, however, and especially those in rural areas, are unable to meet their own expenses. Their children are

These elderly men are enjoying board games in Yongdu-san Park in Busan. The elderly comprise a significant and growing proportion of the population.

burdened by higher costs of living (Seoul is the seventh most expensive city in the world to live in) and many find it difficult to offer support to their ageing parents.

A national pensions scheme has been established to try to support workers when they retire, but this is as yet not fully developed. As a result, people continue to work into their late 60s (longer than in some other developed economies) in order to afford to live. Health experts believe the South Korean government can no longer rely on traditional family support and needs to do more to prepare for its ageing population. Another consequence of South Korea's ageing population is a potential shortage of working age people (15 to 64 years) to support the population. South Korea will either have to invite immigrants to replace the declining working population or expect people to work for longer before they retire.

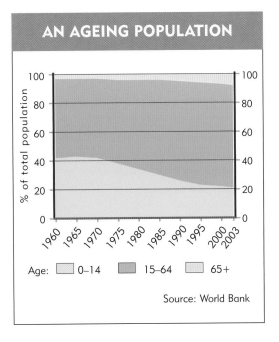

AN AGEING POPULATION

Age: 0–14   15–64   65+

Source: World Bank

A group of young children enjoy a pre-school day out in Seoul. There are concerns that not enough children are being born to provide for the future needs of an ageing population.

ONE-CULTURE NATION?

South Korea's population is one of the most homogenous in the world, with over 99 per cent of the 2003 resident population being ethnically Korean in origin. The Korean people are related to the Mongoloid racial group, which includes the Chinese and, in total, makes up around 70 per cent of the world's population. This connection means they share much in common with other ethnic groups – particularly those in China (especially Manchuria), Japan and Mongolia, with whom there has been historical contact through trade and conflict. Contact with China, for example, has resulted in over half of the words used in the Korean language being of Chinese origin.

Although remarkably uniform, it would be wrong to consider South Korea a one-culture nation. It is certainly true that Korean culture is strong in its own right, and continues to be well-preserved, but it has also been, and still is, heavily influenced by external forces.

South Korea's population is overwhelmingly of Korean ethnic origin, making it one of the most uniform populations in the world.

Historically, these have been mainly from China, Mongolia and Japan and are seen in language, architecture and the arts. The second half of the twentieth century saw increasing Western influence – partly due to growing trade links, but more specifically as a result of US military presence in the peninsula since 1945. Ten-pin bowling and baseball, for example, have become highly popular activities and numerous American-English words have become part of everyday language.

FOREIGNERS

The number of foreigners living in South Korea has grown rapidly in recent years – both through the influence of closer trade ties with other countries, and the increasing attractiveness of South Korea as a place to live. In 1992, there were only 65,673 foreigners registered as residents in South Korea, but by the start of 2004 this number had increased to 437,014. This still represented less than 1 per cent of the population, but may signify an important trend towards a more multicultural society in the future.

This shoe shop is in the 'Little Russia' district of Busan, where an increasing number of people from the former USSR have settled.

The most significant groups of foreigners living in South Korea include the US military, the ethnic Chinese and a growing Russian population. In 2004, the US military presence in South Korea remained much as it has since the end of the Korean War, at around 37,000 personnel. This is set to decline in the coming years as control of the demilitarised zone (DMZ) between South and North Korea is handed back to South Korea. Ethnic Chinese officially number around 20,000, but it is estimated that tens of thousands more Chinese (perhaps as many as 80,000) work illegally in South Korea with false documents. The Chinese have settled in many places, but especially in port cities, such as Incheon and Busan, both of which have popular Chinatown districts. Seoul and Busan also have areas known as 'Little Russia', because they have attracted a significant Russian population, officially numbering around 10,000. In Seoul's 'Little Russia', however, more realistic estimates put the number of Russians, Ukrainians and others from former Soviet states at around 50,000.

KOREANS ABROAD

The upheaval and disruption of the twentieth century means that many ethnic Koreans have moved abroad in the recent past. There are an estimated 1 million in the USA and Canada, a further million in Russia, 2 million in China and around 0.8 million in Japan. There are also smaller populations of Koreans living in South America and Europe.

These people are learning Chinese script in a traditional school. The Korean language and script is heavily influenced by Chinese.

A rice harvester busy in the paddy fields. Rice is the main grain crop of South Korea and is grown intensively on low-lying and level land.

South Korea has experienced one of the most incredible economic transformations of any country in the last 50 years, shifting from a rural economy based on farming and fishing to one that specialises in heavy industries and hi-tech manufactured goods. It must now consolidate its position and work towards closer regional and global integration if the country is to sustain its economic miracle.

RURAL ORIGINS

Unlike many other economies of comparable size, South Korea does not possess a wealth of natural resources. In fact, besides coal and limestone deposits in the Tabaek mountains, and minor deposits of other minerals (including tungsten, gold, silver, molybdenum, zinc, copper and lead), South Korea is mineral poor. Land and water have, historically, formed the basis of the economy; an economy rooted in farming and fishing. As recently as 1970, agriculture (farming and fishing) employed 50 per cent of the workforce and contributed 27 per cent of national income. By 2001, this had fallen considerably, to around 10 per cent of the workforce and just 4 per cent of national income. Despite this decline, agriculture remains an important element of the economy – worth around US$37 billion in 2002.

FARMING

Rice is by far the most significant crop in South Korea (in 2004, the country was the world's twelfth largest producer of paddy rice, with a total production of 6,351,000 tonnes).

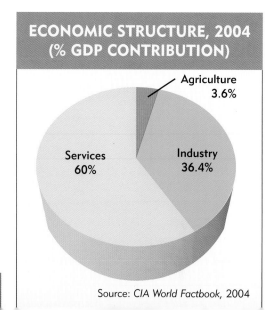

ECONOMIC STRUCTURE, 2004 (% GDP CONTRIBUTION)

Agriculture 3.6%
Services 60%
Industry 36.4%

Source: *CIA World Factbook*, 2004

It is the mainstay of the Korean diet, accounting for 30 per cent of dietary intake in 2002. Other important farm produce includes an incredible variety of vegetables and pig meat (pork). Wheat, barley, beans (especially soybeans), pulses and fruits are also cultivated. The majority of farm produce is consumed within South Korea, but small quantities of higher value crops, such as tangerines, chestnuts and ginseng are exported. Though self-sufficient in rice and some vegetables, South Korea's growing population means it must import an increasing amount of food. In fact, by the late 1990s, up to 75 per cent of South Korea's food crop needs were imported. Farming in South Korea faces a difficult future because of the limited land on which to expand production, and the shortage of labour in rural areas. Domestic farm produce is also facing competition from cheaper produce imported from countries such as China.

Dry farming
Mixed farming
Wet farming
Mixed commercial farming
Island farming

MAIN FARMING AREAS

CASE STUDY
INSAM

The root crop, ginseng, is valued for its use in traditional medicine. South Korea is said to grow the best ginseng in the world.

Ginseng is a root crop believed to have numerous health-giving properties, including the giving of strength and the promotion of fertility and a long life. It is called *insam* in Korean, meaning 'man root', because it is often shaped like a person. South Korean ginseng is considered the best in the world. White ginseng (*baeksam*) is the most common and is harvested after about four years' growth. Red ginseng (*hongsam*) is more valued and is harvested after six to seven years. Because of its health values and the fact it takes so long to grow, ginseng is a prized commodity in South Korea. The government even limits how much is allowed out of the country. Wild *insam* is occasionally found and sells for thousands of dollars.

FISHING

Fishing contributes less than 1 per cent of national income directly to the economy, but its importance far outweighs this figure. Indirectly, the fishing industry encourages many other industries. For example, boat-building and repairs, marine electronics and engineering, net and gear manufacture and transportation and marketing services. The fisheries also provide a vital source of food to the population, helping to ensure food security and reducing the need for imports.

In 2002, Korea ranked as the thirteenth largest marine fishery in the world, producing 1,663,289 tonnes – around 2 per cent of the world total. Inland fisheries are minor by comparison, but aquaculture (the farming of fish rather than catching them in the wild) is significant. In 2002, South Korea's aquaculture production ranked sixth in the world. Over 50 fish species, 15 types of shellfish and various seaweeds are now farmed in marine fish farms. The entire fishing industry employs some 250,000 people, with about a quarter of

these jobs in the growing aquaculture sector. Since 1982, the government has been reforming the fishing industry to create a more sustainable industry for the future. Landing quotas (limits) were introduced in 1987 to preserve stocks and, since 1994, the government has been buying up older, environmentally harmful boats in an effort to reduce and modernise the fishing fleet. In 2002, South Korea's fishing fleet numbered just under 95,000 vessels.

EARLY INDUSTRIALISATION

Prior to the start of the twentieth century, industry in Korea was limited to small-scale cottage industries and crafts producing goods for a wealthy elite. During the Japanese occupation, industries were developed to take advantage of the peninsula's mineral resources, but over 90 per cent were located in what is now North Korea. At the time of South Korea's founding in 1948 there was little industrial infrastructure, and most of this was destroyed during the Korean War (1950–53). In the immediate post-war period, small manufacturing industries were established in South Korea in order to provide clothing,

Fishing is a large-scale commercial industry in South Korea, but fleets and workers are being reduced, due to pressure on ocean stocks.

shoes, household goods and supplies that would otherwise have to be imported. Larger industries, including cement manufacture, energy production, plastics and oil refining, followed to meet South Korea's emerging energy and construction needs. However, it was the first of the five-year economic plans launched in 1962 that really set off South Korea's industrialisation.

EXPORT-ORIENTED INDUSTRIALISATION

With virtually no natural resources, and a small and impoverished domestic market, the South Korean government embarked on a policy of export-oriented industrialisation as a way to promote economic growth. This meant utilising South Korea's plentiful supply of cheap labour and good ocean links to produce goods for the export markets. Initially, this strategy worked well and industrial production grew by an annual average of 17 per cent in the 1960s. Exports, mainly of manufactured goods, increased even faster – at around 36 per cent per year between 1961 and 1972. By the early 1970s, however, labour costs were rising and manufacturing was becoming increasingly mechanised. Relying on exports from labour-intensive industries to boost economic growth became questionable. As a result, the government switched its focus to capital-intensive heavy and chemical industries.

The labour-intensive textile industry was one of the first to help South Korea's economy boom in the 1960s and 1970s. Today, it is less important, but still very productive.

HEAVY AND CHEMICAL INDUSTRIES

South Korea built its heavy and chemical industries by importing raw materials, using its own skilled labour force and rapidly developing technical and engineering expertise. By the end of the 1970s, the heavy and chemical industries accounted for around half of all South Korea's exports. The key industries in this sector were petrochemicals, steel, shipbuilding, automobiles and home appliances.

The Hyundai shipyard in Ulsan is the largest in the world, capable of producing over 70 ships at any one time.

CASE STUDY
SHIPBUILDING

One of South Korea's greatest economic success stories is its shipbuilding industry. From virtually nothing in the early 1970s, South Korea overtook Japan in 2004 to become the world's leading shipbuilder. Of all the orders for world shipping taken in 2004, South Korea accounted for 40 per cent, compared to Japan with 25 per cent and China with 14 per cent. In particular, South Korea has managed to capture the market for specialist shipping, such as tankers for transporting liquefied natural gas (LNG). The three main shipbuilding companies in South Korea captured almost 90 per cent of orders for LNG tankers in 2004. Across the Yellow Sea, China's shipbuilding industry is growing fast and poses a threat to South Korea's dominance. To overcome this, South Korean companies are developing new ship designs. One such project involves a super-vessel that could carry 10,000 individual cargo containers. If built, this would be sufficient to transport around 30 million pairs of sports shoes!

South Korea has become a specialist at producing hi-tech LNG tankers, such as this, for transporting liquid gas across the world.

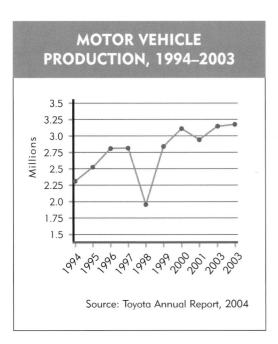

MOTOR VEHICLE PRODUCTION, 1994–2003

Source: Toyota Annual Report, 2004

production plant in Slovakia, capable of producing 390,000 cars a year.

STRUCTURAL REFORMS

By the early 1980s, South Korea had emerged as one of the leading newly industrialised countries (NICs) in Asia. The NICs of Asia (including Singapore, Hong Kong and Taiwan) became known as the 'Asian Tigers' due to their phenomenal economic growth, but by the 1980s their position was being challenged by new emerging economies. In order to maintain economic growth, South Korea underwent a series of structural reforms to its economy. These reforms were designed to make international trade easier, but they also opened up local markets to foreign produce and so challenged the position of local suppliers. In response, the South Korean economy improved its efficiency so that its goods remained competitive in international markets. The government also recognised the need to encourage investment in industrial technology as the computer generation and a greater degree of automation was fast approaching. These changes transformed the economy yet again and by the mid-1980s South Korea was emerging as one of the world's leading hi-tech economies.

Heavy and chemical industries remain a significant element of South Korea's economy today and many of the companies involved, such as Hyundai, Daewoo, Kia and Samsung, have become household names across the world. Having established themselves in South Korea, several of these companies are now looking overseas in order to further expand their business. For example, in 2004, the car producer Kia agreed a deal to invest in a new

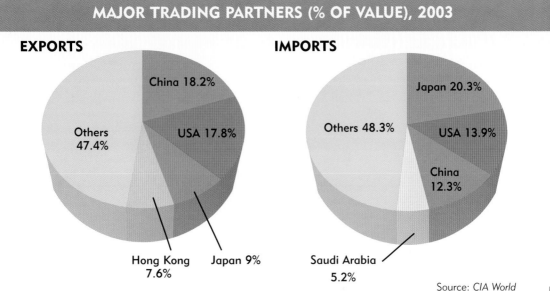

MAJOR TRADING PARTNERS (% OF VALUE), 2003

EXPORTS

China 18.2%
Others 47.4%
USA 17.8%
Hong Kong 7.6%
Japan 9%

IMPORTS

Japan 20.3%
Others 48.3%
USA 13.9%
China 12.3%
Saudi Arabia 5.2%

Source: CIA World Factbook, 2004

THE HI-TECH ECONOMY

South Korea's hi-tech industry is focused on consumer electronics, computers, telecommunications and electrical components, such as semiconductors. As with its heavy industries, several of South Korea's hi-tech companies have become leading global brands – for example, Samsung and LG (Lucky Goldstar). Samsung has been particularly successful in the mobile phone industry and, in 2004, it sold 86.5 million phones (a 55 per cent increase on sales in 2003), accounting for 13.7 per cent of the global market. With its semiconductor and other sectors also expanding in sales, Samsung made profits of over US$10 billion in 2004.

The success of South Korea's hi-tech industry is attracting overseas companies to locate in, or source components from South Korea in order to take advantage of its highly skilled workforce and expertise in this sector. The US companies Hewlett Packard and Motorola, for example, both purchase memory chips from Samsung. Other companies, including IBM and Microsoft, Sony and Phillips, have close ties with South Korea's

CASE STUDY
LG ELECTRONICS

LG Electronics is among the world's leading electronics companies, employing some 64,000 people in 76 countries. It has established global market leadership in numerous electronic products, including air conditioning units, optical storage devices (CD and DVD writers), DVD players, microwave ovens and vacuum cleaners. It is also among the top five producers of monitors, digital displays and mobile phones. LG has set itself the target of becoming one of the top three global electronics companies by 2010, and with sales more than doubling between 1998 and 2003 (mostly due to export sales), it is well placed to achieve this. In the fast-changing world of technology, however, research and development of new products is essential to staying ahead of the competition. To this end, LG is leading the development of technologies that expand the capabilities of mobile phones and is also exploring the idea of 'home networking'. This allows home appliances, such as the television, dishwasher, air conditioning, microwave oven, and even the vacuum cleaner, to be controlled from a single console. It would even be possible to communicate with the appliances remotely by using your mobile phone. You could come home to a perfectly warmed house, with your favourite music playing and your dinner already cooked!

These appliances are part of a new 'home network' technology being developed by LG Electronics.

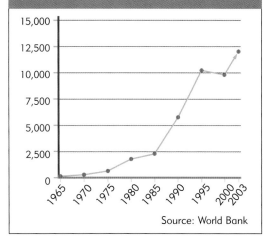

Source: World Bank

hi-tech companies. A group of 13 German universities is even establishing a joint Korea-German Institute of Technology (KGIT) in Seoul. When completed in 2008, KGIT will allow these two hi-tech economies to share research and development in areas such as information technology, nanotechnology and biotechnology.

SERVICE INDUSTRIES

As South Korea's economy has matured, an increasing proportion of the labour force has been employed in the service sector. This sector includes industries such as banking, insurance, retail, tourism and transport, as well as general office work. In 2001, the service sector accounted for 62 per cent of employment in South Korea and 61 per cent of national income. The sector can expect further growth in the coming years, as higher disposable incomes and greater leisure time amongst South Koreans leads to an increased demand for their services.

'Lotte World' in Seoul combines retail and leisure facilities in a single complex. A growing number of service industry complexes such as this are being developed in South Korea.

FEMALE LABOUR FORCE (% OF TOTAL)

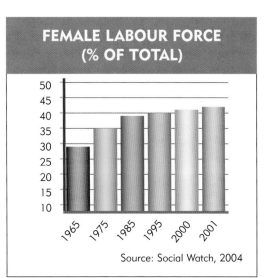

Source: Social Watch, 2004

INTERNATIONAL TOURIST ARRIVALS

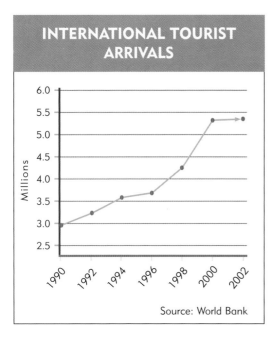

Source: World Bank

TOURISM

One of the newest growth sectors in the South Korean economy is tourism. Cheaper international travel and growing prosperity amongst South Korea's neighbours (especially China and Japan) have helped to almost double the number of international tourists visiting South Korea between 1990 and 2002. Domestic tourism by South Koreans has also increased dramatically, to the extent that 70–80 per cent of the population makes more than one visit a year to one of the country's major tourist areas.

The majority of tourism in South Korea focuses on the country's cultural and natural assets, both of which the government is active in preserving. The Korean Folk village near Suwon, for example, has been established as a living museum to celebrate and preserve historical lifestyles and traditions. Tourists can explore traditional Korean homes, watch traditional craftspeople at work and enjoy displays of traditional dancing and acrobatics. Elsewhere, national and provincial parks have been established to protect regions of natural beauty, whilst opening them to controlled tourism. Bukhan-san National Park on the

CASE STUDY
INSADONG

The growth in tourism (domestic and international) in South Korea has prompted many cities to develop specific tourist districts. One of these is Insadong in the capital Seoul. A mainly pedestrianised area of the city, Insadong retains many old buildings that have today been turned into traditional restaurants and teahouses. Curio shops, art galleries, antique stores, street stalls and public entertainment are also found here. The area is popular with foreign and local tourists, and is also a trendy place for Seoulites to hang out and escape the buzz of the city.

Tourists hunt for Korean souvenirs in the popular tourist district of Insadong in Seoul.

SPORTS TOURISTS

South Korea's tourist industry has been boosted by the country's hosting of major sporting events. Seoul staged the Olympics in 1988 and, in 2002, South Korea and Japan jointly hosted the football World Cup Finals, an event that attracted an estimated 150,000 tourists.

A mural painted on a construction fence commemorates the 2002 football World Cup Finals, when South Korea went football mad. The event attracted thousands of new tourists.

outskirts of Seoul, and Seorak-san National Park near Sokcho, are among the most visited national parks, attracting annual visitor numbers of around 4 and 5 million respectively.

Another popular tourist destination is the island of Jeju-do off the south coast of the peninsula. Known as the Hawaii of Korea, because of its beaches and palm trees, the island offers a complete escape from the more frantic pace of life on the mainland and is only an hour's flight from Seoul. Besides its beaches and the impressive volcanic scenery of Mount Halla-san, the island has traditional working villages and a popular conference centre that hosts national and international events.

A *harubang* (village guardian) at the Seongup folklore preservation zone on Jeju-do – one of the island's top tourist attractions.

JEJU-DO

Jeju-do is such a popular getaway that there are 55 flights a day between Seoul and Jeju City (the capital of the island). A further 46 daily flights link Jeju City to other cities on the mainland.

The South Korean currency, the won, had to be devalued during the Asian economic crisis of 1997, and has not yet recovered its former strength.

ECONOMIC OVERVIEW

Having had four decades of strong and virtually uninterrupted growth, South Korea's economy suffered a major setback in 1997 that threw it into a period of crisis. Foreign investors had, up until this point, poured millions of dollars into the economy of South Korea and other emerging Asian economies in the hope of 'cashing in' on their incredible economic performance. The financial sector in many of these countries was not fully regulated, however. This resulted in large sums being invested in high-risk and poor-quality investments. In 1997, investors in

Thailand began to withdraw their money as they realised the economy there was under-performing. This created an atmosphere of uncertainty and panic across South-east Asia that quickly spread to South Korea. Investors withdrew millions of dollars, companies were facing financial ruin and thousands of jobs were lost as businesses closed or restructured. The impact on the economy was dramatic. The South Korean won plummeted in value from a 1996 exchange rate of around 800 won to the dollar to 1,400 won by 1998. Unemployment more than trebled from 2 per cent in 1996 to 7 per cent in 1998 (as high as 15.9 per cent among 15–24 year olds). The net result of the crisis was that South Korea's economy actually contracted in 1998 by almost 7 per cent.

The financial district of Seoul, where many jobs were lost during the economic crisis.

Recovery and Reform

The International Monetary Fund (IMF) stepped in to prevent South Korea's financial crisis spiralling out of control. It set up a series of reforms aimed at restoring confidence in the markets of South-east Asia. South Korea was quick to implement the necessary reforms and, in 1999, the economy registered economic growth of 9.5 per cent. Growth has continued ever since, albeit at a

Consumer confidence and increased high street spending show that South Korea's economy is back to full growth following the 1997 economic crisis.

slower rate than before the crisis, and by 2003 unemployment had fallen to around 3 per cent. The economy is well on the way to full recovery, but reforms to the banking and business sectors continue, in an effort to avoid a repeat of the 1997 crisis.

CASE STUDY
YELLOW SEA ECONOMIC BASIN

One of South Korea's recovery strategies following the crisis of 1997 has been to look at closer regional economic cooperation. This would strengthen and diversify the economy, make it less vulnerable to future shocks and less reliant on single large markets (the USA being a major market for South Korea). The Yellow Sea Economic Basin (YSEB) is one such regional project in which South Korea is playing a central role. China, Japan and North Korea will join South Korea in making up the nations of the YSEB, a region extending 200km inland from the rim of the Yellow Sea. In total, the YSEB has a population of over 200 million

people, including 60 cities of over a million. In 2001, the YSEB had a potential market valued at US$1.3 trillion. South Korea is developing New Songdo City on an area of reclaimed coastline as the centrepiece of the YSEB (see page 21). With major port facilities and Incheon International Airport on its doorstep, it is hoped New Songdo City will become a key hub for the YSEB. If successful, the YSEB will rival other economic powers, such as the USA and the European Union. But such success is dependent not only on creating the necessary infrastructure, but on overcoming political differences between the member countries.

ENERGY AND TRANSPORT

The bright lights of Seoul by night are a clear indication of South Korea's energy consumption.

South Korea's rapidly growing economy places enormous strains on the country's infrastructure as higher living standards demand more energy and better transportation. In a country that is 70 per cent mountainous, and with few natural energy sources, this presents a considerable challenge to the government.

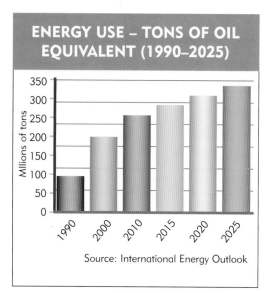

ENERGY USE – TONS OF OIL EQUIVALENT (1990–2025)

Source: International Energy Outlook

ENERGY HUNGRY, ENERGY POOR

South Korea is an energy hungry country, driven by the unparalleled growth in its economy and the rise in personal incomes. Between 1970 and 2001, for example, average energy consumption per person increased by 788 per cent. This compares with an increase of 66 per cent in Japan, 7 per cent in the UK, 5 per cent in the USA and a decline of 10 per cent in Denmark over the same period. For an energy hungry country, South Korea is lacking in significant energy sources. There are deposits of coal in the Taebaek mountains, but these are of low quality and only suited for domestic heating. Hydro power is harnessed for electricity production on the country's major rivers but, in 2002, contributed only 1.1 per cent of total electricity generation. The bulk of South Korea's energy must, therefore, come from imported sources.

ENERGY DEPENDENCE

In 2003, South Korea was the world's fifth largest net importer of petroleum and the world's second largest importer of liquefied natural gas (LNG). These two energy sources account for approximately 55 and 10 per cent of total energy consumption in South Korea. Coal accounts for a further 21 per cent – again nearly all of it imported. This makes South Korea highly dependent on world energy markets to meet its energy needs, and vulnerable to changes in world prices. In order to overcome the problems of energy dependence, South Korea is investing in numerous energy projects. Within South Korea, for example, there has been heavy investment in nuclear energy since 1977 to replace coal and oil-fired power stations. By 2004, there were 18 operational nuclear power stations and several more in various stages of construction.

NUCLEAR POWER

Electricity generated by nuclear power in South Korea is expected to increase by 70 per cent between 2000 and 2020.

South Korea is also investing in energy resources overseas, in an effort to secure energy supplies for the continued growth of its economy. The Korean National Oil Corporation (KNOC) has oil production fields in Argentina, Peru, Yemen, Venezuela, Libya, Vietnam and the North Sea. By 2010, the government has stated that KNOC should supply 10 per cent of the country's oil needs. The state power company KEPCO (Korea Electric Power Corporation) also has investments in several Australian coal mines, providing a substantial proportion of South Korea's total coal demand.

All of South Korea's petrol must be imported, making it very vulnerable to fluctuations in global oil prices.

RENEWABLE ENERGY

Besides limited hydroelectric power, South Korea has no significant sources of renewable energy. Solar power is receiving considerable attention as the technology becomes cheaper and more efficient. In Daegu, for example, Kyungpook National University is pioneering a 'solar campus' to demonstrate the capabilities of different solar technologies in meeting future energy needs. Solar power is also being used in small-scale operations, or remote locations where it can be the most cost-efficient form of generating electricity or heat. Wind power is also expanding, though from a very low level. In 2002, there were just 11 wind farms (or individual turbines) – with the majority being on Jeju-do. Being a peninsula, however, South Korea has considerable wind potential due to oceanic winds – particularly in the south-west and the southern islands. By 2004, new wind power schemes were under development with German and Japanese companies that have expertise in this area.

ROAD TRANSPORT

As with many developed economies, higher incomes have led to a boom in car ownership in South Korea. By 2001, there were some 8.9 million cars and a further 3.7 million trucks and buses on the country's roads. The majority of these vehicles have been added since the 1980s. The number of cars per 1,000 people has increased from just 6.5 in 1980 to 48.4 in 1990 and 171 by 2000. This incredible

GRIDLOCKED

South Korea's road traffic density (vehicles per km of road) is around 120 – double that of Japan and the UK, and four times that of Denmark and the USA.

growth means South Korean roads are today extremely busy, and congestion, accidents and traffic-related pollution have become major issues.

South Korea's road network has expanded rapidly since the 1950s and today covers around 87,000km. The most important roads in the country are the 2,000km of expressways that radiate out from Seoul to other major cities. These also link other key cities, such as Ulsan and Busan in the south. The expressways were begun in 1967 and mostly completed by 1976. They had a dramatic impact on the country, bringing every point of the nation to within 24 hours' travelling time. This allowed greater movement

This new facility – being built at Nanjido on the outskirts of Seoul – will create energy from the city's waste.

of industrial and agricultural produce. It also promoted higher levels of urbanisation, as people could move to the cities with considerably greater ease. Road construction continues apace in South Korea, with new urban expressways in major cities and new

A network of expressways head out of Seoul, connecting it to other cities in the country. This one follows the route of the Han River.

highways linking to more remote regions of the country, such as the mountainous east.

CASE STUDY
HOP ON THE BUS

Buses provide the main mode of public transport for intercity transport in South Korea and an extensive and frequent system covers all major routes. Express services have limited stops and are designed to offer fast transit between key towns and cities. They radiate out from Seoul along the country's expressways and are mainly used as a cheaper alternative to the train. Intercity bus

services use regular (not expressway) roads, and are either express services with limited stops, or regular services stopping at any point and all towns on route. These intercity bus services are especially important to people living in rural areas and to the elderly, as these groups are often in the lower income bracket and so less likely to have their own private motor vehicle.

Bus services are one of the most popular forms of transportation in South Korea, providing vital links to those places not on the rail network.

RAIL NETWORK

The rail network in South Korea is constrained by its geography – and so is located mainly in the less mountainous western and southern portions of the country. This is also where the majority of the population lives. By 2004, the total network covered 3,388km, including new lines built to carry high-speed KTX trains that began running between Seoul and Mokpo and Busan in March of that year. It is hoped that the KTX services, which can travel at 300km per hour, will help to revive the loss-making railway system in South Korea. Passenger numbers are not a problem, with demand rising by around 60 per cent over the period 1994–2004, but the rail system has been unable to cope with this. The new KTX trains and routes are predicted to allow a 340 per cent increase in passenger capacity from 180,000 per day to 620,000.

URBAN RAIL

In 1971, Seoul began construction of a subway (metro) system to provide fast and efficient travel across the city, and to relieve congestion from the city's roads. The system has now grown to cover close to 500km of track split across eight lines, with further lines (and extensions to existing ones) planned by 2010. The system is fully automated and is used by millions of people every day. Busan, Daegu, Incheon and Daejeon have all

TRANSPORT NETWORKS

— Main road

····· Railway

✈ International airport

followed the example of Seoul and introduced subway lines to cope with their own urban transport needs. Hi-tech trains are also being developed for 2010. These will travel up to 30 per cent faster, allowing greater utilisation of the rail network and therefore higher passenger numbers.

Metro (or subway) systems provide the easiest form of transport in South Korea's larger cities and the networks are expanding rapidly.

INTERNATIONAL LINKS

With the land link to Asia blocked by North Korea, South Korea's international transport links are by sea and air, and both are very well established. Sea links are predominantly for freight cargo but, as well as providing for international shipping, they also link the mainland to South Korea's numerous islands. The principal ports include Busan (the fifth busiest port in the world), Pohang, Incheon and Gwangyang – with others, such as Tonghae, Mokpo and Jeju also being important. Facilities at the principal ports are among the best in the world for container and bulk cargo handling, and their usage continues to grow dramatically. Between 2000 and 2002, for example, the volume of

The main container port in Busan is the busiest in the country and one of the busiest in the world.

container freight handled increased by 28 per cent. The equivalent growth in the USA and Japan, by comparison, was just 5 and 3 per cent respectively. Passenger ferries operate from many of South Korea's ports, serving island communities and providing an important tourist route to Jeju-do. Larger ports also provide international ferries to China, Japan and Russia.

South Korea has an extensive internal and international air network, with 7 domestic and 8 international airports. Seoul is the primary air-hub, served by two international airports – Gimpo and the newer Incheon that opened in March 2002. Built on reclaimed land, Incheon International Airport is one of the world's largest, and has ambitions to become the air transport hub of north-east Asia, with more than 60 cities of over a million people within 2 hours' flight time.

An Asiana Airlines (one of Korea's two main carriers) plane at Incheon International Airport prepares for a long-haul flight to London and New York. Incheon is a state-of-the-art airport built on reclaimed land and is set to become a major transport hub in eastern Asia.

Office workers socialise during a lunch break in central Seoul.

The pace of change in South Korea's economy and population has had a profound impact on the daily lives of Koreans over the last three decades. Housing, health, education, leisure, and cultural values have all changed dramatically. Yet amidst this change, South Korea's past is still very evident, and traditional values, such as close-knit families remain strong.

FAMILY VALUES

The family has traditionally been the foundation of Korean communities. Families lived in the same house or nearby, under the guidance of the eldest male, who was respected and obeyed by all below him. Upon his death, the role of family leader would pass to his eldest son and so on down through the male side of the family. Females were historically less valued as they left their birth families upon marriage to become part of their husband's family. Rapid industrialisation and urbanisation in South Korea has led to a weakening of the geographical proximity (closeness) of families, as different members have become dispersed across the country in search of job and housing opportunities. The social role of the

A bride dresses in traditional *hanbok* for her wedding. Weddings are a big family occasion and the trend for traditional style ceremonies is on the increase.

family remains strong, however, and the patterns of respect and obedience continue, even over distance. Families still get together regularly – especially for key annual festivals such as *Chusok* (the harvest moon festival), and family events such as weddings and *Tol* (the celebration of the first birthday that was a significant milestone before modern medicine improved infant mortality rates).

SENSE OF COMMUNITY

South Koreans' sense of community extends well beyond the family. They are well known for being very friendly and sociable people. Even everyday tasks, such as travelling to school or work, or shopping, are done with company. Almost everywhere you look, people are in conversation, sometimes with people they have only just met. In many other societies, the pressures of modern urban life have tended to erode (weaken) such strong social bonds, but in South Korea there is little sign of this. South Koreans (especially the younger generations, as in other countries) have also been adept in using modern technology, such as mobile phones and text messaging, as another form of socialising.

The press in South Korea is free and very active. Most adults will look at a newspaper at some point in the day.

Family values even form the foundation of South Korea's most successful businesses – the chaebols. A chaebol is a conglomerate of companies that form part of one giant parent company. In South Korea, the chaebols include Samsung, Daewoo, Hyundai and LG. Most of South Korea's chaebols have developed from family-run businesses, with the parent company headed by the father, and the various sons (and other relatives) running the subsidiary companies. The government invested heavily in the chaebols as a way to encourage economic growth, but by the late 1990s it became clear that the chaebols had too much power. They not only controlled the largest manufacturing businesses, but also owned banks, housing corporations, social services, insurance companies, transport and tourism facilities. The government is now reforming business practices to allow others to compete with the chaebols, but the chaebols and their families still dominate almost every aspect of the economy.

45

The Seoul National University Hospital is South Korea's main hospital and was founded in 1885. It employs over 3,700 people and serves around 2.25 million patients in a year.

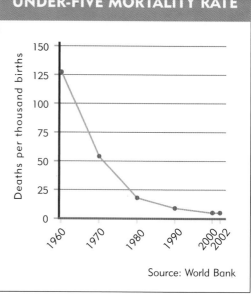

UNDER-FIVE MORTALITY RATE

Source: World Bank

HEALTH AND WELL-BEING

South Koreans today enjoy a standard of healthcare comparable with that of other leading industrial countries, such as Japan, USA, UK and Denmark, but many of the improvements are comparatively recent. In 1960, for example, when other industrialised nations already had life expectancies of around 70 years, South Koreans could expect a lifespan of just 54 years. By 2002, life expectancy had increased to 78 for women and 71 for men. Other health indicators have shown similar progress, such as a fall in infant mortality (children dying before their first birthday), from 9 per cent of live births in 1960 to 0.5 per cent by 2002.

EDUCATION

Free and compulsory education up to the end of middle school (16 years of age) has ensured South Korea has a well-educated population, with almost universal literacy. Education is highly valued and considered by most Koreans to be the best route to success. The government spends around 21 per cent of its budget on education, compared to just 4 per cent in the UK and only 2 per cent in the USA. The school system is similar to that in other industrialised nations with pre-school (5–6 years of age), elementary school (7–12 years), middle school (13–16 years) and high school (16–19 years). Virtually all children complete education through to high school

CASE STUDY
TRADITIONAL MEDICINE

Though modern medicine is widely available in South Korea, a considerable number of people continue to use traditional medicine known as *hanbang*, meaning 'Korean prescription'. *Hanbang* draws heavily on Chinese remedies and practices that were introduced in the sixth century. Acupuncture (*chi'im*), pressure point massage (*chiap*) and herbal remedies (*hanyak*) are among the different techniques used. *Hanyak* is particularly interesting and involves dozens of different natural ingredients from roots, leaves, bark and fungi, to nuts, fruits, honey, deer antlers and dried centipedes! Each remedy can involve the mixing of dozens of ingredients and follows a series of prescriptions contained in *Tong-ui pogam*, a 25-volume medical book first published in 1610. The ingredients are sold at traditional medicine pharmacies (*hanyakbang*) and at a select number of herbal markets. The largest of these markets are Yangyong Shijang in Daegu, which accounts for around 40 per cent of all traditional medicine sales, and Gyeongdong in Seoul.

and, from there, around 70 per cent will go on to higher education (college or university).

In addition to the formal education system, many children (and adults) take extra lessons, such as language courses. English is one of the most popular languages, as it is associated with better job opportunities. Language schools are found in almost all major towns and there are even English language resorts, where young Koreans can go to stay and live in an all English-speaking environment.

OFFICIAL LANGUAGE

In 2004, Samsung announced that by 2008 it would adopt English as its official language, in the belief that this will improve its business opportunities.

All children study at elementary (as here) and middle school and most continue through to higher education.

TELEVISION SETS (PER 1,000 PEOPLE)

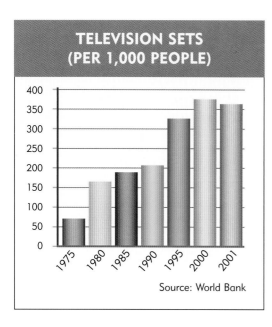

Source: World Bank

TELECOMMUNICATIONS DATA (PER 1,000 PEOPLE)

Mainline phones	489
Mobile phones	679
Internet users	552

Source: World Bank

Ten-pin bowling is a popular pastime in South Korea.

LEISURE TIME

A shorter working week and higher disposable incomes have led to a boom in leisure and domestic tourism in South Korea. Improved health and the ageing of the population have also contributed to these industries, as an increasing number of Koreans enjoy a more active retirement. Among the older generations, South Korea's numerous historic palaces and its beautiful national parks are particularly popular. City workers also seek these quiet refuges and, on fine weekends, the paths in more popular parks can seem almost as crowded as downtown Seoul.

Eating out, meeting in coffee bars, browsing around the shops, and going to the cinema are all popular activities amongst young South Koreans. Cinema has become so popular that an annual film festival was founded to celebrate Korean movies and the best of the foreign-made films. The Busan International Film Festival attracts huge audiences and many international stars. There is even a walk of fame, where film stars have left their handprints. In such a hi-tech society, computer games, amusement arcades and the Internet are replacing many other forms of entertainment. In 2004, South Korea had the world's highest distribution of broadband Internet networks. The popularity of

computer-based entertainment has led to concern about rising rates of computer addiction amongst younger people.

SPORT

South Koreans enjoy keeping fit and it is common to see people jogging, skating or cycling in city parks or exercising in public gymnasiums. The most popular sports in the country are football and baseball. Football received a huge boost when South Korea co-hosted the 2002 World Cup Finals with Japan. The unexpected success of the South Korean team – who made it to the semi-finals – sent the country football crazy. South Korean athletes also excel in badminton, and their archers are the best in the world, carrying on a tradition in archery that dates back thousands of years. The traditional form of archery called *gungdo* is still practised, along with other traditional Korean sports such as *ssireum* (wrestling) and *taekwondo* (a form of martial art).

Enthusiasts practise traditional archery, called *gungdo*, at one of the only remaining ranges in Seoul. It is now protected as a culturally important site.

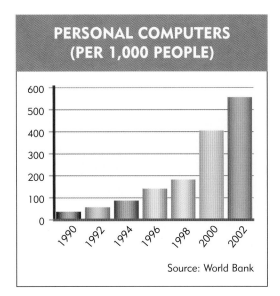

PERSONAL COMPUTERS (PER 1,000 PEOPLE)

Source: World Bank

CASE STUDY
CYWORLD

In 2004, there were an estimated 23.8 million 10–39 year olds using the Internet in South Korea. The main use of the Internet is for online gaming and cyber chat, and a number of companies have become specialists in meeting the huge demand. Cyworld is the most successful of these, with over 10 million members since it was set up in September 2001. Cyworld offers users their own mini homepage, known as a 'hompy', where they can place pictures, music, games, and web content, and a chat room to meet real or 'virtual' friends. Each hompy also includes a 'mini-room', which users can decorate with items bought from a cyber shop that also sells music and games. A new currency – acorns – has been created to purchase items in Cyworld, with one acorn being equivalent to 100 won (9 US cents). In October 2004, Cyworld was earning 150 million won a day from acorn sales alone.

TRADITIONAL CULTURE

In recent years, Korean culture and its unique traditions have enjoyed a resurgence. Traditional weddings are on the increase and so is interest in traditional sports. In fact, nearly all aspects of Korean culture are being re-examined by the present generation and carefully preserved for those of the future. Tourism has been an enormous boost to such efforts, generating interest in Korean practices from paper-making and traditional dance, to costumes and food.

AN ACQUIRED TASTE!

Korea's unique cuisine is based upon the historical availability of food supplies and, although many Western foods are now widely available (especially fast foods), local dishes are still dominant. Being surrounded by water, fish and shellfish are a major part of the diet and are normally eaten as soups, side dishes or dried snacks, rather than as a meal in itself. Meat has become part of the Korean diet in more recent times, with beef, chicken and pork all widely eaten. *Bulgogi* (thin strips of marinated beef) and *bulgalbi* (marinated beef ribs) are particularly popular, and Western fast food companies have even created *bulgogi* burgers to appeal to Korean taste buds.

The two staples of the Korean diet are rice (as boiled rice or various forms of rice cake) and *kimchi* (or *gimchi*). *Kimchi* is a seasoned and fermented vegetable – normally cabbage, turnip, radish or cucumber – that is eaten as an accompaniment with virtually every meal. There are around 200 varieties of *kimchi*, using different ingredients in the seasoning process such as garlic, chillies, salt, clams and anchovies. Winter *kimchi* was traditionally made in clay storage jars. These were partially buried, to keep the fermenting ingredients at just the correct temperature. This process allowed vegetables to be eaten right through the winter months, and *kimchi* jars are still in use today.

Kimchi (pickled and fermented vegetables) is considered the national dish of Korea and is available in hundreds of forms.

THE PAST ON SHOW

Many aspects of Korean culture are today largely for show. It is rare, for example, to see traditional dress (called *hanbok*) unless it is worn as part of a cultural performance or ceremony. Traditional dance and music, such as *Nong-ak* (farmer's dance and music), is nowadays mainly performed at cultural shows for tourists. Most of South Korea's traditions are exhibited in cultural villages, such as the Korean Folk Village near Suwon, but, in one or two places, whole villages have been declared 'folklore preservation zones'. Here, people continue their lives as part of a living exhibit. One such village is Seongeup on Jeju-do, where traditional village guardians (*harubang*) still protect a cluster of around 300 traditional buildings from evil spirits. Besides the traditional construction materials of stone walls and thatch-roped roofs, local customs are still used. Each house, for instance, has two stone posts at either side of the entranceway, with three holes in each to hold poles that span the entrance. If all three poles are in place it means no one is home, so please stay away. If the top pole has one end lowered to the ground, the owners will be back soon. If all three poles have an end lowered it means they are at home and you are welcome.

The traditional farmer's dance is one of the most popular shows at the Korean Folk Village near Suwon.

The gate poles of this traditional Korean homestead signal that the owner is home.

Rush hour in Seoul produces such traffic jams that, as in other large cities, air pollution is a major problem for the health of people living there.

The pressures of economic expansion and a growing population have taken their toll on South Korea's environment. There are problems of water and air pollution, habitat destruction and overuse of water resources. But South Koreans also show a strong appreciation of natural environments and flock in their thousands to the country's wilderness areas and national parks.

POLLUTION

South Korea's intensive use of resources for rapid economic growth creates various forms of pollution. In terms of air pollution, for example, South Korea emitted more carbon dioxide (one of the major greenhouse gases) into the atmosphere than all but seven other countries. In context, however, this was still only 8 per cent of the amount emitted by the USA, and in per capita terms (counting each person) emissions are below the average for the OECD nations. With rising vehicle use and growing energy demands, South Korea is taking measures to meet its future energy needs, whilst minimising any increase in carbon emissions. The investment in nuclear energy, for example, eliminates the carbon

dioxide produced by burning coal or natural gas. Vehicles are also being converted to run on auto-gas, rather than petrol or diesel, as it produces far fewer emissions. This includes a government scheme to replace 20,000 diesel buses with natural gas buses by 2007.

Agricultural chemicals are a major source of water pollution – South Korea has one of the highest rates of fertiliser and pesticide use in the world. In 2003, an estimated 36.9 tonnes of nitrogen fertiliser and 1.43 tonnes of pesticide were applied per square kilometre of agricultural land. This compares to an application rate of less than 12 and 0.25 tonnes respectively in countries such as Denmark, UK and the USA. During the 1990s, the government began to acknowledge that water pollution had become a major problem. Chemicals from agricultural and industrial waste (including dangerous heavy metals such as cadmium and mercury) were contaminating water used for drinking and for watering crops. In 1998, the government introduced new water management measures that, by 2004, had seen a halt in the decline of water quality in the country's main rivers. The government is creating new policies for a water conservation project to take place between 2006 and 2015. This will include new limits on the acceptable levels of pollutants entering the water system.

Cardboard is collected from stores and restaurants in Seoul and taken to be sold for recycling.

CASE STUDY
SUSTAINABLE CITY

In 1978, the Nanjido district of Seoul was chosen as the landfill site for the waste generated by the rapidly growing city. An area of wild flowers (Nanjido means 'flower island'), wildlife and lakes became a massive mountain of waste, with 93.5 million tonnes of industrial and municipal waste dumped there by 1993. This mass of waste created two massive plateaus over 90 metres high, and turned local streams into stinking polluted wastelands. In 1994, a dramatic turnaround began at Nanjido. The plateaus of waste were stabilised and covered to form parkland and wilderness areas. The waste also provided a source of energy – by tapping and using methane gas produced by the decomposing waste. Sustainable technologies – such as wind turbines and solar power – are being pioneered on the site, and recreation and education facilities encourage visitors to live a more sustainable lifestyle. An environmentally friendly residential area will complete Nanjido's transformation from waste dump into a model of sustainable living.

Haneul Park in Nanjido is today a haven for wildlife and city dwellers, but was until recently Seoul's biggest landfill site.

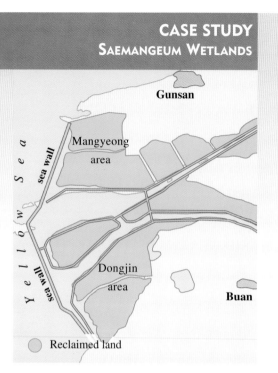

Gunsan

Mangyeong area

Dongjin area

Buan

Yellow Sea

sea wall

sea wall

Reclaimed land

South Korea's most controversial environmental issue is the reclamation of the Saemangeum wetlands between Gunsan and Buan in the west of the country. The wetlands are an important habitat for birds and fish species, including around 20,000 migratory birds that rest here on their journey between Australia and East Asia. Some of the bird species at Saemangeum are listed as endangered – for example, the spotted greenshank, of which there are fewer than 1,000 left in the world. Plans to reclaim Saemangeum for agricultural land

were passed in the mid-1980s, with the intention that the new land would help meet growing food demands. The massive 33km sea wall that would enclose the wetlands began to be built in 1991. By 2005, it was nearing completion, with less than 3km to finish. Environmental groups are concerned that the wall will disrupt the natural ecosystem, and that the drainage of the wetlands will destroy habitats and ruin the livelihoods of local shellfish farmers. Protests by environmental groups have periodically halted construction work at Saemangeum and forced the government to review the whole project. The government insists, however, that the project is environ-mentally friendly and will create new habitats for wildlife and recreation. It is argued that the additional farmland is essential to South Korea's future, as more and more land is engulfed by urban development. The outcome of Saemangeum (the world's largest ever reclamation project) – if and when it is completed – will be closely monitored and may well determine the future of other planned land reclamations in South Korea.

The Saemangeum wetlands at low tide stretch for miles, with the rising sea wall visible in the distance. When completed, this wetland will become fertile farmland.

PROTECTED AREAS

As early as 1967, South Korea recognised the need to protect its most fragile environments. Between then and 1988, the government established 20 national parks. Altogether, these cover around 6.6 per cent of national territory, with a further 1.2 per cent being protected in the form of 22 provincial parks and 31 country parks. The Korea National Parks Authority was established in 1987 to manage the parks and introduce conservation programmes. These programmes include the careful monitoring of visitor impact and, if necessary, the temporary closure of some paths and park areas. With over 25 million visitors in 2003, the national parks have a unique opportunity to help encourage more sustainable ways of living. In 1999, an Environmental Education Programme was introduced to use the assets of the national parks to educate visitors (and especially children) about the value of nature, and methods of conserving it. The programme holds nature experience classes, organises nature-monitoring contests, and works with environmental groups to tackle specific issues of concern.

🌲 National park

🐋 National marine park

NATIONAL PARKS

SPECIES RICH

Although the national parks cover less than 7 per cent of South Korea's area, 70 per cent of the nation's 50,000–60,000 plant and animal species live within them. These include several endangered species such as the moon bear, otter, Korean red-headed woodpecker, brown serpent and longicorn beetle.

Tourists stream through the entrance to Seoraksan National Park during the annual showing of autumn colours in October – one of the busiest times of the year.

Welcome! 즐거운 탐방되세요! 歡迎光臨!

Economic success has brought a world of coffee bars, fashion and technology to young Koreans, but the economy must now keep up with fast-emerging China.

At the start of the twenty-first century, South Korea is entering a stage of maturity that will present its people with fresh challenges. The financial crisis of 1997 signalled the end of the country's honeymoon period and provided a shock to economy and people alike. The signs are that the Korean people are using their characteristic resolve and determination to overcome these challenges, but they know that others lie ahead.

FRESH COMPETITION

South Korea has firmly identified itself as one of the world's biggest economies and a major source of specialist engineering, consumer and electrical goods. It has overtaken countries such as Germany, the USA and Japan and come to dominate key sectors. However, it now faces perhaps its biggest challenge yet from China, one of its nearest neighbours. China is fast emerging as a major economic power and enjoying annual growth similar to that of South Korea in its boom years. The Chinese government is investing billions of dollars into its industries, and utilising the country's vast natural resources and cheap labour to undercut many of its competitors. It has already announced its intention to replace South Korea as the world's number one shipbuilder by 2015, and is fast closing in on the lucrative electronics market, too. The government and businesses in South Korea recognise the threat posed by China and are seeking closer cooperation with China through initiatives such as the Yellow Sea Economic Basin (see page 37). Through building regional cooperation in this way it is hoped both nations can prosper.

SOCIAL CHANGE

The ageing of the population will present South Korea with difficult choices in the coming years. It will need to consider how to care for the older generations and also how to fill the void left in the younger working-age population. Economic immigration (especially from China) is one likely solution, but this could have profound and unforeseen effects on Korean culture. The government has been clamping down on illegal immigration, as it is aware that migrants may threaten the supply of Korean jobs and raise unemployment.

UNIFICATION

The biggest challenge to the future of South Korea is the whole question of reunification with North Korea to form a single Korean nation. The idea of a unified Korea seems almost universally popular in South Korea, but major obstacles and five decades of suspicion stand in the way. Talks between the two Koreas have stalled numerous times, because of suspicions that North Korea is continuing to develop its nuclear weapons programme. North Korea denies this, but has been uncooperative with international monitoring teams. The greatest fear for South Koreans is that the tension over North Korea's nuclear status could lead to another conflict on the peninsula; a conflict that could threaten millions of lives and severely damage South Korea's incredible achievements of the last 50 years.

South Korea's military remain on high alert in readiness to defend any attack from North Korea.

Aquaculture The farming of fish or other aquatic goods (seaweed, shellfish etc) in artificial ponds or large enclosures submerged in the sea and/or lakes.

Biotechnology The manipulation of natural species for human gain. Includes cross-breeding of plants and animals (hybridization) and, more recently, modifying genes using genetic engineering.

Capital-intensive An industry or economic activity in which the use of machinery and equipment is a vital factor, and often replaces or reduces the need for labour. The modern automobile industry is an example of this, with hi-tech robots carrying out the work that was formerly done by several people.

Chaebol A Korean term given to a large business empire (conglomerate) that is normally connected to a single family.

Chemical industry An industry that produces chemicals for the agricultural, medicinal, manufacturing, domestic and industrial sectors of the economy.

Cinder cone A cone of debris that forms around the vent of a volcano during an eruption.

Cold War An ideological struggle between communism (led by the USSR) and capitalist free-market democracy (led by the USA) that lasted between 1945–91.

Consumer electronics Electrical products, such as computers, cameras, televisions, DVD and CD players, and household appliances that are consumed by the general public.

Cottage industry A small-scale industry employing just a few people at a local level. Often related to traditional crafts, such as pottery, paper-making or weaving.

Demilitarised zone (DMZ) An area between South and North Korea established along the ceasefire line between the two countries in 1953. It is approximately 248km long and 4km wide, and acts as a buffer between the two opposing military forces.

Ecosystem The contents of an environment, including all the plants and animals that live there. This could be a garden pond, a forest or the whole Earth.

Floodplain The area of a river system that would naturally flood in periods of high river flow. Floodplains are typically in the lower sections of a river, and are wide flat areas with fertile soils due to the rich sediments deposited during periods of flooding.

GDP (Gross Domestic Product) The monetary value of goods and services produced by a country in a single year. Often measured per person (capita) as GDP per capita.

Geological uplift The process by which land is forced upwards by geological movements and processes in the Earth's crust. These can include volcanic activity and the collision of the Earth's tectonic plates.

GNI (Gross National Income) The monetary value of the goods and services produced by a country plus any earnings from overseas in a single year. Often measured per person (capita) as GNI per capita.

Heavy industry Large and often key industries, such as steelworks, shipbuilding, and construction and engineering.

Homogenous Being uniform or very similar in nature. In South Korea, this is often applied to its population.

Hydroelectric power (HEP) Electricity generated by water as it passes through turbines. These normally involve large dams across river valleys that form artificial lakes behind them.

Immigrant A term used to describe a person who has recently immigrated (moved into) a new area (normally used at the country level).

Industrialisation The process by which a country becomes more industrial in nature and moves away from an economy based upon agriculture or resource extraction.

Infrastructure The lines of transport and communication necessary for an economy and society to function efficiently. These include road, rail, electricity lines, water pipes, sewers, telephone lines, ports, airports and so on.

International Monetary Fund (IMF) An international organisation that assists governments during periods of economic uncertainty or shock by providing them with financial loans. The IMF is designed to encourage a stable world economy.

Labour-intensive An industry or economic activity in which labour (people) are the crucial factor. Traditionally, many industries depended on labour for their success and so could be called labour-intensive.

Land reclamation The process of turning an area (often a wetland or shallow coastal region) into useable land for agriculture, settlement or other economic activity. This is normally done by drainage or infilling.

Lava tube A tubular structure that acts as a vent for volcanic lava to travel upwards to the Earth's surface.

Migrant Someone who has moved into or out of an area – the process of migration.

Nanotechnology Using technology at a very small scale to perform specialist functions.

Newly industrialised country (NIC) Term used to describe a number of economies that emerged during the 1970s in Asia and South America as rapidly industrialising countries.

Silver towns Settlements where retired South Koreans are moving to enjoy their later years. They have the necessary practical and leisure facilities, such as shops, health clinics and golf courses.

Subtropical Climatic conditions that are tropical for part of the year or almost tropical for the whole year. Subtropical regions often support vegetation more normally found in tropical regions.

Sustainable technology Technology that brings benefits to people today without damaging the environment for future generations.

Temperate A term used to describe the dominant climatic conditions found between the latitudes of the tropics and the polar circles. Within this zone, great variations in temperature can be experienced.

Tidal ranges The range of a tide between the high and low tide marks. In South Korea, the west coast has a very large tidal range, but on the east coast it is very slight.

Typhoon A violent tropical storm in the western Pacific Ocean. Known as a hurricane in other parts of the world.

FURTHER INFORMATION

BOOKS TO READ:

Culture In: North and South Korea by Melanie Guile (Heinemann Library, 2004)

Next Stop: South Korea by Fred Martin (Heinemann Library, 1999)

Lonely Planet Guide: Korea by Andrew Bender (Lonely Planet Publications, 2004)

Moon Handbook: South Korea by Robert Nilsen (Avalon Travel Publishing, 2004)

Korea: A Walk Through the Land of Miracles by Simon Winchester (Penguin Books Ltd, 2004)

Opposing Viewpoints: North and South Korea by William Dudley (Greenhaven Press, 2002)

WEBSITES:

CIA World Factbook
http://cia.gov/cia/publications/factbook/geos/ks.html
The US Central Intelligence Agency's online factbook, with statistics and assessments of all countries of the world.

Korea National Statistical Office
http://www.nso.go.kr/eng/
Useful statistical information about all aspects of Korea. Presented in English and clearly organised.

Seoul Metropolitan Government
http://english.seoul.go.kr
Plenty of informative content about the South Korean capital.

Television Trust for the Environment (TVE: News)
http://www.tve.org/news/doc.cfm?aid=1190
Information about the Saemangeum wetlands and the project to reclaim them for agricultural and industrial use.

Korea National Parks Authority
http://www.npa.or.kr/eng/main.htm
Information and statistics in English about the parks service.

USEFUL ADDRESSES:

Embassy of the Republic of Korea
60 Buckingham Gate
London
SW1E 6AJ

Korean National Tourism Corporation
3rd Floor
New Zealand House
Haymarket
London
SW1Y 4TE

Numbers shown in **bold** refer
to pages with maps, graphic
illustrations or photographs

Detail from a drum used during
the changing of the guard at
Changdeokgung (Palace of
Illustrious Virtue) Seoul.

A giant Buddha dominates the
Shinheung-sa temple complex
within Seoraksan National Park
in the north-east of the country.

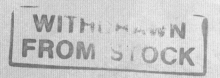